Spectres of God

theology **MY**

Rachel Mann

Spectres of God

Theological Notes for a Time of Ghosts

Fortress Press
Minneapolis

SPECTRES OF GOD

Print ISBN: 978-1-5064-8441-9
eBook ISBN: 978-1-5064-8442-6

Cover design: Kristin Miller

Contents

Introduction

THIS IS A SHORT book about spectres. Lest you think you're reading a book about the occult rather than God, let me add this: this book concerns, to use a familiar and often-used phrase, 'the ghosts of my life'.[1] I have come to understand my theological thinking as a concerted engagement with a series of spectral and ghostly manifestations and traces centred around God, bodies, language, and lives lived through the line of fragility and otherness. I've realised that much of my theological work has focused on unpacking the implications of God's spectral presence in all we are and do.

I know that in talking in those terms, I might

[1] My first encounter with this phrase was c.1981 when the art-pop band Japan released their classic song, 'Ghosts'. It has, of course, since been used by the late Mark Fisher, perhaps the writer who has done most to popularise the word 'hauntology'.

9

put you, the reader, off. Please persevere. I want *Spectres of God*, most of all, to be a place of encounter. I love language and its poetic and resonant possibilities and where I avoid a utilitarian or analytical approach it is because I want to take language seriously. Words matter. Words spark off each other and when I write, I write in search of just the right words. That can feel a forlorn quest, but the search is always revealing. So, when I use words like 'hauntology' or 'precarity' I ask only that you remember I use them because I think they gesture towards something that *matters*. I hope you come to trust my linguistic flourishes.

At the same time, I think the ideas contained here are (in essence) simple. That is certainly true when I manage to say something of God. God is simple. Though, of course, that's the problem we have with her ... him ... them ... We are not adequate to the divine. Human beings are messy and fragile and, more often than not, bewildered. We have a gift for getting lost. We are creatures of language and context and impaired community. 'Sin' is one way of saying that we are so wrapped up in ourselves that we cannot see God right. The delight and wonder of God lies in how he empties himself into flesh in Jesus Christ. God dwells with us in mess and in the bewildering strangeness of body, yet does not get lost; in God, simplicity and its endless resonant riches dwells with us. This is so exciting and yet so tricky for us. How do we even begin to articulate the Living God?

More than that, how can one even begin to articulate the Living God in a time (certainly in post-industrial societies like ours) when – with the best will in the world – the language of God and Church and faith has little or diminishing traction? Yes, the traces of God and the Bible can be found everywhere: in language, in tradition, and so on. God's grammar echoes; the Word – God's first verb – still whispers (and makes things happen), but ... but ... while I believe God is only in mid-articulation, who's listening? In a place like the UK, we are post-God. We know only the power of spectres. We are past the point where most people care about God's sweet articulation.

Perhaps you begin to see why I want to speak of the spectral. In part, it reflects the fact that my background is a little messier than that of some theologians. I came to faith in my mid-twenties having been intellectually formed in an avowedly secular philosophy department around the time 'post-modernity' broke out of the Academy and became fashionable. If God was still around in the Academy I knew him as a series of traces which haunted the history of thought. Furthermore, I am a trans woman who has spent decades negotiating the ever tricky waters of gender, sex, sexuality, feminism, and queer theory. I have lived a world disenchanted and re-enchanted. I have lived in the midst of some of the liveliest discourse of the past fifty years. As a theologian with that kind of backstory and formation, is it surprising that I'm alert to the places where meaning 'fractures', where echoes rebound, and the traces of older dispensations come alive? My world (our world?) feels both enchanted and disenchanted and re-enchanted, and if God so often seems utterly alive to me, I live with his ghosts and spectres too.

What are these spectres? These are, in part, the ghosts of this nation's theological, linguistic, and cultural inheritance. A few years ago, I wrote a book, *Fierce Imaginings*, in which I examined the way the Great War has become a spectral presence in so much UK political and cultural discourse. The book notes how that war's rituals not only are embedded in cultural discourse, but work as a kind of endless return and repetition haunting a society's self-understanding. As I shall try to make clear, these repetitions and returns are not limited to the way twentieth-century wars remain with us. Just when one thinks this society is done with God, there she is again.

In various books, I've examined how versions of God haunt us. None of these versions are benign, especially the holy ones. Some – such as the ever-beguiling Patriarchal God – are downright pernicious. Famously, Nietzsche wrote, 'I am afraid we are not rid of God because we still have faith in grammar.'

Christian theological thinking is deeply embedded in Western philosophy, cultural modes, and language. God's grammar – both good and bad – haunts our cultural ideas and productions (from ideas about forgiveness, purity and righteousness, etc.), to the kinds of stories we like to tell. At their simplest (though often most potent), these mythic stories are reflected in popular redemptive narratives such as the *Harry Potter* books or the *Marvel Cinematic Universe*; at their richest, they are known through tender and measured imaginative explication, critical re-imagination, and even disavowal.[2] Indeed, the very way many current cultural disputes are framed indicate Christian obsessions with righteousness, soundness, purity and rightness.

I know I have personal skin in what might be called 'hauntology', this study of spectral presences and absences. Before I came to

[2] See, e.g., Francis Spufford's *Light Perpetual,* or the work of Marilynne Robinson, the 'Catholic' novels of Graham Greene, or Flannery O'Connor, Dostoyevsky, et al.

faith I felt haunted by God and Jesus Christ. I became convinced that, for all my attempts to achieve escape velocity from God, he would not let me go. I felt the repetitive need to pray. I could not ever quite be avowedly secular (whatever that means, anyway). The world was charged with divine spark. I caught God's mysterious presence out of the corner of my intellectual, emotional, and physical eye. This book takes seriously the idea that humans are attuned to spotting the Divine, even when that comes down to no more than a sense of God as the one who departs as you enter a room. I want to suggest that mystery is embedded in the structure of the universe. I want to suggest that God is unsolvable mystery. I want to go further, though: one horizon of that mystery is that it is possible to encounter Love and Passion inscribed into a seemingly indifferent universe. God is both absolutely present and yet seemingly is condemned to be absent. Part of the reason for God's absence is that we, the noisy species, get in the way. We are the creature that takes up space. Is it hardly surprising that God rarely gets a look-in?

Perhaps this condition of being sure of God and yet alert to his absences is simply the fate of those of us who come to faith late and carry within us the hard-to-shake suspicion that not so long ago it was possible to live a more confident and complete version of the Christian narrative than is now available. Perhaps, as I suspect, this condition affects many more than just us latecomers to faith: it is a broad cultural mode of the current iteration of Christianity.[3] Even if Christianity was never so confident as I imagine, even if such a belief is myth, it is a tempting one. This sense of 'belatedness' provides its own temptations: to be shrill or bumptious – utterly insistent on the power of God's redeeming work – or to sit in the shadows waiting, hoping, and praying that others will catch-on to the beauty and terror of the Divine Mystery. Or, again, one is tempted to get stuck into social action, perhaps hoping someone will ask us why we do what we do and

[3] Which, as Rowan Williams famously notes, might yet be an early rather than a late version of Christianity.

16

give us an excuse to explain our motivations. *Then* we shall reveal to them this wondrous God whom we serve![4]

Either way, I am left with the fact of my complete commitment to something which the vast majority of people in a nation like Britain – if they have a reaction at all – now find irrelevant, implausible and, perhaps, ridiculous. Perhaps even dangerous and, in essence, toxic. More often than not, Christian faith is greeted with indifference. One finds oneself standing up for ways of living in the world which have fallen away into parody or irrelevance; which are seen as yawn-inducingly sad or pathetic. God isn't even in the margins. He is the ghost at another person's feast. He has no credibility. Everyone knows all his moves before he makes them. He's had his time.

If Jesus Christ remains the defining icon of God in our society, then he seems to be in

---

[4] Perhaps what each of us does too little of is dare to be with others – of faith and none – as people prepared to receive news of their encounters with the Beyond or Other in the midst.

pretty poor shape. He has become a symbol among a plethora of symbols: insofar as he is represented by the Cross it is unclear that he has any more 'consumer awareness' than McDonald's 'Golden Arches' or the Apple logo. He has to compete in a consumerist world, one icon among many (and one which seemingly lacks the more immediate benefits promised by most consumer products). To survive, the Church finds itself adopting the language and style of consumer commerce. It sells Jesus. For many, 'Jesus Christ' has become something one exclaims when one is irritated. He gets read through the cultural tropes of the day: Zombie Jesus or Buddy Jesus and so on. At best he offers moral example and advice. He is a counsellor, a wise man, a good guy. A bore? The serious older brother who tells you to stop being a dick. He is, seemingly, no longer the regulatory icon of a culture and hasn't been for an age.

Perhaps it is time to let God go. Perhaps one should simply note the ripples and the echoes of the old ways; perhaps like children with sparklers at a bonfire display we should enjoy the traces of God's sparks for as long as they scar the air. Perhaps one should treat God and Jesus as kindly ghosts, no more scary or effective or real than those ghosts that walk the halls of stately homes; as something only known in the material items – the churches, the baptism silver, the books – that were theirs before they departed. Perhaps. However, I don't think God and Christ are done with us yet. I want to explore the good news of Jesus Christ through some of his spectral presences. The God who dies will not stay dead. His traces – in Christ – lead us back to the promise and hope inscribed in the World.

And, why *spectres*? Well, here's the rub. Spectres have impact, even if they are shadowy. I want to show how the spectral is a material, effective, and affective matter. The spectres of God are no idling ghosts. Even as one struggles to articulate something about, for example, 'God's body', one should not imagine that one cannot encounter it. Spectres have impact. They touch and change us. They direct us to fresh ways of going on. In one's encounters with the spectres of God one can become at peace with limitation, precariousness, lack of certainty, and one's fragility and fractures. Equally, one can find in divine fragility the hope of the world. In three short chapters (on the body, on love, and on time) I want to explore how God invites us, repeatedly, to live in a rich three-dimensional mystery which subverts the depressing flat-earth of modern life. This mystery reveals, to our surprise, a world rich with purpose at every point, even as it troubles us. One finds that to be human holds together the truth that we are made in blessing, live in complexity, and called into promise. If life is lived as tragedy, its ultimate arc is comedy. The ghosts of God whisper that the world has the strangest and queerest beginning, middle and end. Ultimately perhaps the oddest gift of religion is the claim that the world might, just might be structured thus, if only we could believe.

The spectres of God I have known are disruptive; not as poltergeists are disruptive, but as the holy must always be disruptive. God is unafraid of our attempts to domesticate his mysterious, awe-inducing reality. The Word of God is firstly verb because he, she, they, is action, and their action is a making of World which queers, makes strange, and which eludes our desire to stage-manage God. So often we want to direct God so utterly that he moves only on our carefully-programmed cue. The Word of God brings World to birth and, in the Spirit, sustains it. The Living God invites us into the truth that shall set us free and insofar as I can articulate that truth it is as 'mystery'. Just when we think we have the body or time or love and grace sorted, God breaks free. Our death dealing is met with God's resurrection. God shows us the Way.

1

The Spectre of the Body

Surely there is nothing more substantial, simple, and straightforward than a body. I mean, isn't there an *obviousness* to the body? When faced with scepticism about reality, one might – like an old philosopher friend did – tap one's fist on an arm or a leg, on one's tummy or breast, and say, 'Look, this I know ... this is real and solid.' There is surely nothing spectral about bodies or 'the body'. It is the one thing which tells us assuredly that we are here. That we are caught up in now. When pain sears or love blooms we know it through the line of the body.

In this chapter, I want to examine some of the theological and cultural conceptions of bodies which mesmerise me, and indicate how Christ's body – that remarkable, chastised and serially-exploited body – might offer some ways of treating with the mess and glory of embodiment in a world haunted by patriarchal, hetero- and cis-normative and ableist shadows. For what is clear is that not all bodies are treated as equal and as worthy of respect; indeed, all of us – sometimes as a result of ingesting overly-constrained representations of God and Christianity – are haunted by spectres that value some bodies more than others. When one embraces a queered picture of bodies one begins to see the limits of those terrifying works of haunting. Indeed, one begins to see how God invites us into something Other, richer, and more disconcertingly holy.

It is important, of course, to acknowledge that the body has a problematic status in many Christian traditions. Too readily and inappropriately 'body' has been translated into 'flesh' – in St Paul's sense – and too often the body has been seen as the icon of death or the means through which sin is transmitted. It has been marked down as frail and precarious and changeable, as if these are sinful things in and of themselves, and as if the body offers only a means through which sin should be resisted. Through these theological moves, women – coded as frail, changeable, necessary for procreation, etc. – have been overly identified with the body and, in turn, the bodily overly identified with 'the feminine'. The body has been demeaned as marked with 'death'; it has thereby been treated as the enemy to overcome. The Christian faith has too readily praised souls and minds, as if they were separate from bodies.

The bodies which have been taken seriously are those which seemingly approximate ideas that have come to haunt western culture: bodies which are active and able, un-diseased, self-willed, white, straight, independent, obviously powerful, and male. Muscular. There is no space here to explore precisely how this body came to haunt our social structures and cultural imaginaries, but it is a spectre that won't let us go. It has formed and been formed by difficult to foreground aspects of faith, religion and culture. However, it is not difficult to give some examples of the way this idealised body haunts and mesmerises us. We know it is there because we know which bodies get written off or mocked and shamed and treated as other. I know the power of this idealised body because I know what it is to have lived the fact of a body 'falling short'. My queer, trans, femme, ageing and blobby body fails, except in being coded as 'white' and educated, to conform to any of the ghostly ideals which swim around your head and mine.

These ghostly manifestations of bodies really do matter. To reiterate: it is worth calling them spectres precisely because they are no mere ideas or concepts which one can summarily dismiss in argument or by fiat. These spectres have genuine effects and affects. They live in and between our bodies and in the social and cultural structures through which we are formed. They have force and drive us; they cannot be seen except in their effects and affects. There are bodies which we live which are not our own and yet are our own. For example, one looks at one's body in a mirror and judges it fat, thin, pretty, ugly, good, bad and so on and so forth; one lives one's body as if it is essentially separate and discrete from others, and one internalises codes of virtue or wickedness and begins to live up or down to them. Insofar as one's body does not fit the norm it is treated as heretical or problematic or dangerous.

I am not suggesting that it is easily possible to live without these introjects or norms; one cannot simply choose to live outside these ghosts. However, I think it crucial to be alert to their wellsprings and the way in which these ghosts are contingent; as theologians, part of our vocation is to expose these ghosts for what they are – sites of haunting which can be exorcised or at least reappraised. The serious theologian is an exorcist. In this regard her work is attuned to the work of Jesus. There is a work to which we are called that entails casting out demons. It is simply the case that for the last few millennia the work of exorcism has been directed (often with the vilest results) at the wrong targets. The proper targets are the spectres of what Elisabeth Schüssler-Fiorenza calls 'kyriarchal' thinking.[5] In interrogating these spectres, we make room for God's new thing. Perhaps an example of how bodies are haunted sites might make this point clearer. I could talk about so many bodies – trans bodies, female bodies, black bodies, classed bodies, fat bodies, disabled bodies – but I shall talk about the ghost of the able bodied, healthy body which has shadowed my experience of chronic ill-health.

It is worth noting that there are clinically identifiable horizons to chronic illness. There are times when I just am in pain or when my disease is in an active or acute phase. I am exhausted or lose weight and so on. I am someone with a permanent stoma that almost constantly pumps crap into a bag outside my body. My gut is exposed to the world and it bleeds and bleeds. However,

---

[5] 'Kyriarchy' relates closely to the more familiar 'patriarchy'. However, by framing oppressive structural nexuses through the biblical and classical concept of 'Lord,' Schüssler-Fiorenza broadens the frame to show how the language of God intersects with the 'Law of the Father'. Her term covers not just 'lordship' and the 'Father Principle,' but critiques the use of 'whiteness', 'straightness', 'able-bodiedness' etc. as norms.

chronically-ill bodies also have to live with the spectral bodies they have 'ingested'. These are ghosts generated by a culture mesmerised and driven by the ghosts of 'wellness', 'better', and 'health'. In this regard, Susan Sontag makes a helpful distinction between the 'kingdom of the sick' and the 'kingdom of the well'. This distinction is value-laden: the kingdom of the well is the one of which we're all supposed to want to be part; it is also defined, in no small measure, by assigning some to a place beyond its borders in the land or kingdom of the sick.

When one becomes chronically unwell and/or disabled, one can, as illness or limitation draws on, feel increasingly assigned to this kingdom of the sick from which some never return. This kingdom is defined as simply 'bad', cut off from all the good things that come to healthy and better (and morally 'good'?) people; it is a kingdom it is okay to enter for brief excursions,[6] but those who are 'trapped' there

[6]   Indeed, to have travelled briefly into the kingdom of the sick and returned 'whole' might be lauded as 'character building' or as 'inspiring'.

31

– through chronic mental or physical illness – are lost. Not only are they seen with suspicion by those who are well and good, but those who are sick must live with the spectre of 'wellness' they carry in their head. They have to live with illness as well as the sense that such a thing is a judgment on them too, only re-appraisable if that which has been lost – wellness – is recovered. In short, one must overcome or 'fight' this sickness and become 'better'. The only way to 'lose' this fight is in death. One then might be assigned the status of 'good' because one fought 'so hard' to be better.

I do not wish to mock those who want to organise their bodies through the language of struggle, fight, and overcoming, or deny the power of the 'well/sick' dynamic. I feel the power of the spectres too. I've often been praised for 'how well I handle and overcome my problems'. My sense, however, is that a richer vision of bodies is available and that that vision may be drawn from a body so readily ignored in our society that it is seemingly nearly lost: Christ's body.

There is joy in knowing that God, in Jesus Christ, takes our embodiment seriously. Christ knows fragile flesh. He knows dependency and relationship. He knows the leakiness of bodies. He knows we are water and blood and mucus and mess from the outset and that it is good. He enters the world head-first and crying. He knows we are mess as much as we are ever ordered and neat form. He knows that we hold, within our beauty, the possibility of 'meat', of being torn apart and rendered inhuman. He knows the promise we hold in our wreckage. Ultimately, in the Easter Event, he knows the violence of others which tears bodies apart and discovers, in resurrection, there can be dignity, dare I say it 'promise', in scars and wounds which never fully heal.

From the outset, in his formation, the One who Saves is never himself alone, never separate and discrete. He is held in body and amniotic sac. And, though he knows the reality – the reality we all know – of being pushed out of the relational womb into the separation of a fragile and frightening world, this is no God who comes down from heaven in a chariot or is simply an avatar of a Greek god. He begins in dependency and grows in the company of humanity. He is nurtured by his mother and learns from her. Mary, as the one who sings the Magnificat, is the one who surely teaches him to speak the Beatitudes.

The body, conventionally, is a site of nine openings. As a person with complex Crohn's, I have had to learn to live with additional openings into my body. I live with insides on the outside. I live with shit and stench and I have come to know that to accept this reality is not only life-saving, but a place of goodness and gift and hope. It is a place of new, potentially troubling understandings of the world, of truth and the jarring possibilities of lived reality. Herein is part of the adventure of the body: of its precarious promise and its fragile hope, which I think is the only hope that should interest us. Why? Because this is the hope God reveals to us in his punctured body.

God himself, in Jesus Christ, becomes

the site of puncturing. God knows human openings, of course. He knows how the world gets into the body. He knows the places where the costs and pleasures of being mortal issue forth and are received. In Christ, God weeps through *punctum*, the tear ducts. He breathes and speaks and hears and listens. He micturates and defecates. He knows wet dreams. He is pierced upon a cross. In crucifixion, God's body, thereby, becomes a site of five additional openings: the places where nails have pierced skin and bone, and the wound in the side, created by a thrust of a spear. Christ, in his puncturing, is a site of water and blood. If the soldier, in his clumsiness, had pierced the colon or ileum as he thrust his spear up through Christ's body into his lungs and heart, God would also have become a site of stoma.

I guess I'm suggesting, then, that the Divine Body revealed in Jesus Christ resists the fetishisation of the 'well body' which haunts our society. God's solidarity is with real bodies, in their precarity and limitation.

He has no fear of what bodies are and what they may become. Christ's body goes with us into the kingdom of the dead, and into the kingdom of the unlovely and the traumatised. I am minded too of Grünewald's painting of Christ as a plague body, a sick body being crucified. God embraces our real, embodied stories where we are and as we are and here's the shattering truth: he raises them up. Resurrection is not the work of 'wellness' or 'better', but of lifting up and transfiguration in the promise of God's Third Day. This is not a valorisation of pain and violence; it is God situating herself in the midst of the facts, and revealing promise.

As we witness in Christ's risen body, the wounds and openings, the trauma and sickness are not erased. They are brought into fullness and wholeness, in mystery and strangeness, beyond our ready categories of 'well' or 'sick'. There is mystery here which eludes. There is something spectral which is not so much haunting as inviting. God is just out of sight, beyond reach, but we know she is good and exposes this world's ghosts for what they are. They recede and in their place comes the possibility of participating in something we can barely conceive: the wonder of God's Body.

2

The Spectre of Love

IF GOD RAISES our fragile, strange and particular bodies to an unanticipated dignity, to joy even, why should we care at all? What is it all for? Why, indeed, does God bother? Well, perhaps, because it is only through the line of the body that we may find the prospect and promise of being human. God's delight in the awkward, stubborn particularity of our bodies is a signal of the oldest, most abiding spectre in our sceptical world: the claim that we are made in and for love. Indeed, God's persistence with bodies reveals that at the sustaining, transforming heart of the world is gift, grace, and promise.

I suspect some may say that love is no spectre at all. We see it all the time: in our sexual encounters, in engagements and marriages, in family celebrations, in charity, and in the works of faith. Indeed, one might say

'Love' is so banal and available that we have distilled its celebration into (secular) feasts and festivals: St Valentine's Day (for romantic love) or Christmas Day (for love of friends and family). Love is the motor for so many cultural productions, from poetry through to TV shows and on into cinema and novels. We are culturally conditioned to desire, if not expect, the Happy Ending.[7]

Equally, some others might say that the fact that the language of love is ubiquitous is a reminder of profound cultural anxiety. It shows we live in cultural conditions that lionise love and, indeed, fetishise it, but struggle to foster or produce it. Even worse, that we live in a culture that uses love, especially sentimentalised and romantic love, as a feint for its violence. If love-talk is everywhere it may, then, be a token of desperation, an indication that we live in a time when Christianity – which treats love as the greatest virtue – is itself a series of spectral presences. Love mesmerises because it is a passing culture's most determined fiction: a

[7] More on this in the next chapter.

construction of a cultural inheritance out of time; a call-back to a religion whose lease on the world is up. Christians themselves have again and again – in their abuse, violence, and exploitation – revealed how readily they speak of Love, yet cannot model it.

To claim, as I will, that love – capital 'L' love – is spectral is to embrace, ironically, the claim that 'love is all around' as well as to acknowledge the claims of those who see love-talk as the traces of a vanishing world. It is to claim that Love – and its corollary Grace – go ahead of us and are part of the structural silt of reality, often difficult to discern, and resistant to reductive reasoning. In short, I want to say that Love is the sustaining mystery which invites us – as fragile bodies – into life in all its glorious precarity. I want to say that if we are haunted by the mystery of love it is because it is inscribed in the structure of the world. To be biblical, God is Love. God is the one who calls us back to the truth of relationship. She reveals that we find ourselves being our completest selves when we live in her and in each other and in peace with ourselves. Most of all this is the work of living bodies negotiating time and space with all its mess and fragility. It is a work of indwelling.

When I talk in such terms I feel a frisson of fear, perhaps the kind of thing one associates with 'ghostly haunting' in its familiar sense. Why? Because to speak of Love and God in such terms speaks against the kind of formation almost all of us in our society, whether religious or not, have received. For to speak of the 'spectre of love' in the terms I've used is to suggest that the deepest call on human lives is to be in the hands of others; to be in mutual trust, recognition, receptivity, and generosity; to live in community; to take the risk that the one in whom we have placed our trust might betray us, hurt us, abuse us. This way of talking speaks against the world in which you and I have most likely been formed. This is one which prioritises the individual and her self-direction and her separate needs; one which says be suspicious because one's own interests are not other's interests; one which says resources are scarce and therefore protect your own interests. To talk of the spectre of love defies something that even those of us who are 'into' community must acknowledge: that in so many ways we live as separate and discrete bodies. There is a gap between us. We are not, at first sight, like fungi, creatures whose identities and materiality is entangled in one another and whose edges are difficult to define. We act as if we are 'non-fungible'. Into the gaps between us, pathos and tragedy enter in, and it is a gap which our aspirations to love may fail to bridge or transcend. Our resistance to the 'ecotone' – the fertile edge-lands between us – may condemn us to diminishment.

In order to speak about Love, I also find myself speaking against a world I find it difficult to see beyond: the world of capitalist and consumerist desire. This imaginary says that everything can be assigned an exchange value; it says that profit is the abiding truth; it says that desire can never be satiated, only fed. It says that resources are scarce and that

45

scarcity only adds to their lustre. In *Capital*, Karl Marx quotes Christopher Columbus, 'By means of gold one can even get souls into Paradise.' In our world, even love has an exchange value. As John Berger put it, 'Nothing exists in itself. This is the essential spiritual violence of European capitalism.'[8]

There is another reason to shudder in the face of indwelling conceptions of love: they have been used, in the most violent ways imaginable, to deny and erase the dignity of difference. The repression of difference by Christian communities over millennia, in the name of love, does not need to be unpacked here. It is the shadow which rightly limits any triumphalist account of God's love as community. It is a reminder that there is an appropriate tentativeness and restraint – an attentiveness to the almost spectral threads – when one speaks of love. Faithfulness to God requires asking, 'Who or what is barely

[8]   John Berger, *Notes from a Possible Future*, in 'Steps Towards a Small Theory of the Visible' (London: Penguin, 2020)

seen, yet present? Who are we not including?'
Still I want to stand up for a vision of human
flourishing shaped around the idea that we
have the best hope of being our fullest selves
when we risk being in the hands of others. Yes,
there must be checks and balances on the
communitarian temptation to erase difference
and particularity, but ... I sense those checks
are predicated on daring to embrace a vision of
God's body as strange, and as rich and odd as
that shown in the previous chapter. Community
claims us and forms us, but if one person is
demeaned or rejected for the person they are,
it is impaired community.

Perhaps, then, this is the moment to
speak of the Holy Spirit, the Ghost of Love
herself, who hovers over creation, whose work
sustains, and who gathers us into community
and communion; who works in and between us
and who goes ahead and remakes us in grace.
To speak of her at all is to speak of mystery; it
is to speak with a humble confidence in that
which is most seen in effects and affects. We
witness her in that which is changed and has

been changed. We see her in the rear-view mirror, or as a dot soaring above the horizon. She is at work in the dazzling and glorious dark. Indeed, if the Spirit leads us into all truth, she also leads people into metaphor and, therefore, into play. We reach for words to speak of her – air, wind, breath, fire, and much more. Indeed, I think we shouldn't stop there, but continue to test the limits of language for ways to speak of her. She is in the spaces between and she is one who enables us to recognise that we are never ourselves alone; she reveals how we are beautifully entangled in one another; she is the one who shows that we receive grace from the fertile edges. She is ecology and ecotone. We note her dance most often when she has already seemingly moved on. There is a riskiness and precariousness about the Spirit's work because that work is nothing more than love.

That's all very well, though. Highfaluting language will not address the concrete demands of indwelling love. So here's a way to unpack the spectre of love in a more grounded way: 'compassion'. As many people know, at its root, 'compassion' means 'suffer with'. Henri Nouwen adds this: compassion is nothing more or less than the 'full immersion in the condition of being human'. Nouwen reminds us, then, that compassion takes us to the deepest and profoundest reality of our human embodiment. Compassion embeds the ghost of love in community. When we are compassionate we are caught up in our fullest humanity as those called to embody Love. Compassion, then, surely implies that to be human is all about relationship, entanglement, and connection. For without relationship I can't see how it is possible to 'suffer with' and alongside other humans.

When we, as people, fail to be compassionate or good or loving, it has become something of a modern refrain to say, 'Well, that's because we're only human.' That's precisely what we're not. We struggle to be human. Indeed, I have come to believe that there is a liberating beauty and challenge in acknowledging that there has only ever been one human being, Jesus Christ. The rest of us are approximations. We are sketches. If we were in a movie, we'd be the badly rendered CGI. We are not human, yet. Insofar as we are unable to be compassionate, it is not such that we are being 'human all too human', but not yet human.

The invitation to meditate on the spectre of compassionate love is an opportunity, then, to spend time with the body in the hands of the other, irresistibly and necessarily, in risky entanglement; where, sometimes, the line between bodies is not readily discerned; where blood is sometimes spilled and is freely given; where the edges are fluid and where one discovers that even as we talk of 'my body' or 'the discrete body', bodies are ecological – they hold a gut of love filled with fauna and flora.

Here, again, the body of Jesus Christ is iconic. A way to consider this is in the power of the Easter Triduum, as it takes us from Maundy Thursday through to Easter Day. It gives us permission to reflect on God's body, in Christ, in the hands of others (in extremis); it offers an opportunity to come to terms with our failure to be compassionate and how much we struggle, thereby, to be human. It reveals how the Ghost of Love is grounded in relationship.

Part of the power of the Passion Narrative lies in the way it holds the drama of life: it reveals how the most significant friendships and relationships can end up in the wreckage of betrayal, failure, denial and cowardice. The behaviours of Judas, Peter, and the rest earth the cosmic drama of redemption in recognisable failure. Our failures in friendship and love, which reflect our retreat from the call to compassion, find a place in God's story. The Passion reveals yet more. At its locus is the torture and execution of the Son of God. Perhaps torture and state-authorised execution are the very acme of our species' capacity to suspend and limit compassion and empathy. Ethicists like Jeremy Wisnewski and R. D. Emerick have suggested that, in torturing his victim, the perpetrator renders himself less than human. In short, if the torturer immersed themselves in their full humanity they could not do their job. Insofar as we, on Good Friday, make Jesus our victim, we only reiterate our capacity to circumvent compassion. The Passion reveals us for what we are: the species which can suspend our capacity to 'suffer with'.

Of course the story does not end in crucifixion. Christ's resurrection offers us the promise of a renewed humanity. The violent subversion of compassion represented by the torture and execution of God on the Cross is not the final word. The Living God takes our death-dealing into himself and returns to us in the promise of resurrection. Given our treatment of Christ, it would not be unreasonable to expect the resurrected God to come seeking vengeance or our annihilation. Instead Christ comes towards us in the Garden on Easter Day offering peace and reconciliation and an invitation into a new way of life defined by love for one another. The one who has exposed our violence invites us to become fully immersed in the condition of being human.

I've long adored the fact that compassion

in both Hebrew and Greek has a bodily significance. The ghost of love is earthed in body. The Hebrew word for compassion is *rachuwm*. It is taken from the root word *rechem*, which means 'womb'. When I became aware of the connection between womb and compassion, I felt I had encountered something of the structure of God's first language. I felt as if something of the world's substrate was revealed. This is the God who feels for us in her womb. Equally, the ancient Greek for 'guts' is *splagchnizomai*. One of its implications is 'being moved to one's bowels', which itself means moved to compassion. For in classical culture, the bowels were the seat of compassion and pity. These etymological connections underline how in baptism, as we are born again in Christ, we encounter the compassion of God who feels for us in her womb; they underline how, in Eucharist, we are sustained and renewed as we take God into our guts. To be members of the Body of Christ means that we are people of compassion – of gut and of womb. The spectre of God's love and grace may always be known in embodiment. This is always a gift of faith, known in effects and affects.

To speak in such terms is a reminder that the life of compassion to which God invites us is a costly, embodied one. It is never simply an idea or reducible to good intentions. It entails coming to terms with the violence and cruelty seemingly sealed into our species' DNA, as well as being prepared to live in resistance to such violence. The life of love, of compassion, entails daring to be caught up in this world without simply being crushed by it. If 'passion' has implications, as W. H. Vanstone reminds us, of being 'handed over', 'compassion' entails, in part, embracing that handed-overness. To our shock, the route to life, which is nothing more or less than the life of a human, lies in being part of God's Body. How is such a thing possible? Through the Spectre of Love, the Holy Ghost, who makes the impossible possible. In love, we are called into the ecology of God's body; in love, we are that body.

As we grow ever more into the life of the Body of Christ, we begin to reappraise those things which we thought were obvious. For example, that the world is binaried (men and women, black and white, good and bad, etc.) or that we are mere individuals separate and discrete. I begin to discover that in my flourishing is yours and in yours is mine. One finds that the seeming gaps between us are the edgelands of grace, fertile with promised love and new possibilities; one discovers that this seeming scrubland is more fertile than pasture. One learns that in Christ there is no Greek or Gentile, no male or female or or or ... One comes to know that the promised land of Christ's body is where all shall know *hesed* – blessed and loving kindness – and that there is space for all. As we become entangled in God and one another, we discover the loving, gracious spaciousness of the Kingdom. The Spectre of Love brings us into the fullness of life.

3

The Spectre of Time

STILL, YOU MAY be wondering: The spectre of the body and the spectre of love ... surely they are not enough? To have weight they need to be set in a schema of time and purpose. There needs to be a sense that who and what we are *add up* to something. There is need for a story; a sense of end as *purpose* or *telos*. Perhaps here one meets a defining problem for faith in a time of ghosts: it is seemingly no longer possible to believe in the future.

'What?', you might say. 'No longer believe in the future?' Not unreasonably, you might raise a quizzical eyebrow. You might adduce all sorts of examples of the questing, visionary projects of nations and entrepreneurs as they seek to make science 'fiction' science 'fact'.[9] Or you might meet my statement with a series of other questions: The future? Is that something in which to believe? You might also wish to ask, who is this 'we' of which you speak? Or you might ask *which* future and *whose* future? What does 'believe' mean here, anyway? All good questions. Nonetheless, I suggest that it has become difficult for most, if not all, of us quite to believe that the future holds promise and possibility.

Our human futures are haunted by spectres which, by turn, frighten and exhaust us. Currently the most compelling and frightening spectre is environmental collapse. We grieve that which is yet to happen, not least because we know it is already happening and has already happened. We are caught up in spectres of

[9] Your head might now be reaching for images of the promise held in the idea of 'space exploration'. However, these images are drawn primarily from the 1960s and 70s; our images of space are less ambitious now. Where once we spoke of 'colonising the stars' by the 2020s, we now have visions of billionaires taking joy rides and day trips to just beyond the upper atmosphere. Our futures have grown smaller.

time which bring together past-present-future simultaneously; we are haunted by the past and the present and the future. As children of a visual culture – we live in the wake of cinema, TV, YouTube and TikTok – images lodge in and drive our imaginations. We have been so colonised by the visual that we barely doubt our right to watch and observe everything, no matter what is taking place (bombings, murders ...) and yet we are sickened by it (in every sense). We do not need to live in Brazil to be sure that each day a section of the Amazonian rainforest the size of Wales is destroyed. We do not need to be on a boat in the Pacific to know that vast fields of plastic bottles and detritus coalesce and float on the ocean. These fields of plastic exist both out there and inside our heads. We have become so dependent on these 'organic' products that we suspect our very DNA is changing. Human beings have always been the most plastic of species; now we suspect we are changed by the micro-particles of plastic we cannot expunge.

For the vast majority of people in a society like ours there is a kind of magical abundance of stuff. We have never possessed so much; we have never had such access to the cornucopia of creation. What was once only a dim picture of a future of instant gratification at the press of a button[10] is available, at least at a price. However, in the midst of our abundance we are exhausted too, not least because we are haunted by our own need for the stuff which generates collapse. Our technologised society – defined by the internet, cloud storage, and smart tech – eats up and heats up the earth. As I type on my doody iPad I am aware that my cloud storage is held in some super-cooled facility that, ironically, only adds to the warming of the planet. I want everyone to have access to the digital power I have and yet I am aware that if they did it would only burn through the planet's resources more rapaciously. My privilege is predicated on scarcity and

[10] Think of the utopian visions of *Star Trek's* 'luxury communism'.

exclusion. I feel paralysed. How can I, we, us, escape this system of destruction? One says, 'I want to be good', not least because one is so aware of what is going on EVERYWHERE, all the time, via one's electronic device.

And, sometimes, one has a sense that ecological collapse might be avoidable if one could simply unplug or restart or reset. If if if ... our governments and leaders and all the rest of us could stop fetishising the economic-social nexus of which one is part and on which many of us – including a disabled person like me – depend. But what 'out' is available from this way of living we now know? What other future? Can Marx or God or Jesus really save us? Haven't those futures been foreclosed? One might sing 'This train is bound for glory ...' but one actually believes, 'This gravy train is bound for perdition ...'. The future is now – we hold it in our hands, we obsess over it all day, every day – and that future is the power of a thousand civilisations accessible with a click. One of its uncanny horizons, perhaps even a horrifying horizon, is how very many of the poorer people in our communities have privileges most gods would envy (knowledge and information at the fingertips ...), but still remain hungry. If the future technological vision of the 1960s and 1970s has become ubiquitous, nonetheless people starve and cannot afford decent housing. The utopian dream has gone sour. Crucially, if the future is now, it does not lie ahead. We play out environmental collapse in our heads, not least because the collapse is yesterday, as well as today and tomorrow. The open texture of the world is gone. Something is coming and what is coming is the end. We are haunted by the spectres of a lost future.

How might one even begin to speak theologically into a time of lost futures? Well, one might, not unreasonably, insist that one should simply let tomorrow take care of itself; that the future really can only be addressed by a focus on the present, on 'today'. Or one might say, that as a Christian one's focus on the future should be fixed on the 'eschaton' or the 'parousia': there is only one 'future' worth claiming and that is the new heaven and new earth 'beyond time'. This might strike one as the biblical and theological way.

There are layers of hauntology here, however. While I do not doubt, for a second, the reality of the climate emergency, nor the rationality of reacting to this unfolding disaster with grief and anxiety and fear,[11] it is surely also true that – at the level of cultural imaginary – our sense of impending disaster also represents the latest iteration of the discourse of the 'End Times' or the 'end of the world'. Ideas of the apocalypse are inscribed into Western cultural imaginaries not least because of Christianity. Anticipation of the end of all things is a form of Christian haunting, present in the earliest Christian texts and worked deeply into the texture of Christendom and post-Christendom.

Equally, when I begin to think theologically about time and the future, I find myself with

---

[11] And maybe even with a sense of wantonness and abandon ... 'the ship is going down so let's get very very drunk'. I do *get* that atavistic reaction.

a kind of vertigo and discomfort precisely because I have been formed in a time when Christian ideas about the 'future' hope – about the parousia or about 'heaven' – seem less available. I sometimes think that of all the things one is asked to believe as a Christian, the notion of a New Heaven and New Earth, or of the completion of the world in Comedy, and the Return of Christ in Judgment require the most flex. *And he shall com with woundes rede, to deme the quikke and the dede …* These thoughts, nightmares and visions are among the most unthinkable. I can readily embrace the idea of Jesus's birth, life, death and resurrection; I can live into the Ascension and inhabit the power of Pentecost. But the judgment of the world? The New Heaven and New Earth? In the preface to her commentary on the Apocalypse of John, *The Face of the Deep*, Christina Rossetti writes, 'If thou canst dive, bring up pearls. If thou canst not dive, collect amber.' I feel so overwhelmed in the face of God's Apocalypse that I am quite overwhelmed. I can neither dive nor collect.

I am left with an instinct to try and make it tractable and small – to think of this world as a kind of novel, with, at most, the promise of a sequel. But when I do so, it becomes rather difficult to conceive of life with an open, rich texture. One begins to feel, with apologies to God, like a character in a novel whose plot one might write better oneself.

But still the question of promise and purpose haunt me. Which brings me to the oddest spectre of all: the disturbing, haunting and lingering power of God's time. It disturbs, haunts and lingers because it begins precisely where we don't expect: the starting point is Resurrection or, as I shall call it, the Third Day. Though we have become conditioned to the logic of 'beginning-middle-end', and indeed, when one picks up a Bible one finds a creation narrative on the first page, nonetheless God endlessly queers our expectations. This is the God whose speaking is a making of the world; when she speaks, there *is*. An English translation of the opening of John's Gospel offers this most remarkable construction: 'In the beginning was the Word, and the Word was with God, and the Word was God. He was in the beginning with God. All things came into being through him, and without him not one thing came into being.' In these lines, one senses time stretching and flexing to accommodate the possibilities of God's Word, who was *before*, is *now*, and shall *ever be*, world without end. The Word who is Jesus Christ, was, and is, and is to come.

God's strangest and queerest invitation is to accept that the truest reading of time and future and hope and promise comes when we locate ourselves in the realm of the Third Day. The telling point of adventure is not our human birth, or the realities of being incarnate, or torture and violence and violation, or even death (though all of this matters). The telling point is the news shown forth on the Third Day: the pivot is Resurrection. Reality is 'retconned' in and by the Third Day. Or even more: the Story of God, in which we are invited to participate and locate ourselves, is a reading backwards and a reading forwards in dynamic relationship.

To put it in simple and personal terms: I remember exactly when I came to faith. I was 26. It was Whitsunday, 1996. That day I became a Christian. That is true, but in coming to faith I also encountered a richer gift: the knowledge that I had been a Christian since baptism as a six-month old child. Time and grace work back and forth. In Resurrection one reads back into Passion, and Passion reaches forwards into Resurrection. All blessing is now; all blessing is in the past; all blessing is to come. In the wonder of the Third Day – the Day of Resurrection – one participates in the God whose speaking is creating; Third Day is First Day; First Day is Third Day. One apprehends how gift and peace and promise were inscribed into the very first moment, the First Day, of creation. God's spectral presence in Time simply blows our minds.

This deep present of God, this deep past of God, and this deep future of God breaks open for me ways of reading and being in the world that disrupts our secular and diachronic ideas of time and promise, as well as exposing some of the thinness of overly precise theologies of grace and salvation. Perhaps I am just saying that I am drawn to the disconcerting, spectral horizons of God shown forth in John's Gospel: this is the God who offers eternal life now and yet invites us to know that it is yet to come. But I also want to say that the Synoptic Gospels too hold this *now and not-yet* in their texts and textures. When Jesus says, let tomorrow take care of itself he is not offering advice for those seeking serenity and mindful centering. The Kingdom that is here and is yet to come is no mere rhetorical device. God is about some serious shit that was held in the moment before the moment before the moment of the Big Bang, and we encounter it in hints and glimpses, in affects and effects. In the power of the spectral.

If this cannot be readily comprehended, if this *is* overwhelming, that is as it should be. I am not saying that the world was made in six days; I am not suggesting that the judgment of God and the return of Jesus Christ are precisely captured in the Apocalypse of John. I am saying that words are not adequate to the Word. Our metaphors, our similes, our sentences and poetry and novelising and word-making fall short of the language of God – her verbs, nouns and adjectives, metaphors and similes, of her subjunctive moods, and conditionals, and of the whole excessive, strange and abundant Language of God. In the end, as one seeks to be *kataphatic* – that is to find positive ways to articulate the wonder of the Living God – one ends up in the *apophatic*, the way of unknowing and the way beyond. One ends in silence. The facts of God and the promise of God totally fry our brains. As we encounter God we are undone. She has passed by in the pillar of cloud and leaves us slack-jawed, haunted and dazed.

Is this vision of God's overwhelming, haunting power a recipe for quietism? For some, maybe, a kind of quietism might be just what is required. There are times when I need to acknowledge who and what I am in the grand expanse of God's universe. In being humbled lies the promise of the 'begin-again'. To 'treat' with such an excessive God is an opportunity to divest pretension. In humility, one may be enabled to see the Other as neighbour and act on it. Such encounters will be, for some of us, the bonfire of doctrines and positions we deploy to make us feel safe or better or more righteous. For some of us, a version of God or Jesus or the Spirit that really needed to die will die. Those versions may continue to haunt us and it will take the risen, living God to show them up for the shades they are.

I also know that speaking of time and God in 'spectral' terms might barely seem to address pressing matters of politics and ethics — of how one might act in a world where economic and social futures seem foreclosed, either as a result of climate crisis or totalising ideologies. I am more hopeful.

To embrace, in all its outrageous oddness, the Third Day as the turning point of the world will always be a moment of disruption. It is always a crisis point. It is – for those with more politically and socially charged minds and bodies than mine – a moment for both a new vision and the possibility of a richer politics. To confront a world coming to an end with the gift of God who is World Without End might yet be a moment when poetics transforms politics.

For all of us I hope an ongoing, powerful encounter with the spectre of God's time and reality means that we become ever more the people of the Third Day. As we dare to live the absurdity of the Third Day, we become more human and thereby more divine and vice versa; we share in Christ's humanity and divinity. As we become what we already are – which is human – we become what we already are – which is divine. Consider the very strangeness of that sentence, the oddness of its jarring tense. It tells us about how God's queer time works. We are called to become who we already are. That is the story of the People of the Third Day: we are called to become a community of reconciliation and forgiveness and show how what we practise is marked by the Love, Grace, Peace and Holiness with which we have always been inscribed.

I believe, then, that there is a tenderness to God's time. I hope I say this without smugness or over-confidence. I know only too well, as both a priest in God's church and as someone who remains marked out as 'other' or 'dodgy' or as a 'fake Christian' by so many, that life is rarely lived as comedy and the community of God is a serial perpetrator of violence and hate. I know, in my very flesh, how life can be nasty and pain-ridden and lacking in any obvious future or promise. Still I want to stand up for the tenderness of time, even if to do so seems as insubstantial as a ghost. God's community has the promise of reconciliation inscribed in it, even if it is not now, not yet, but one day. Even if most of us live each day as a constant Ash Wednesday, or an endless Good Friday or as a Holy Saturday, there will be another day. Not just tomorrow, but the day after that. That is the promise of the strangest day. The queerest day. The most outrageous day. The Third Day.

Postscript

A Kingdom of Love (3)

If, in the Resurrection, I shall be raised
To congregation – face-to-face,
All eyeless skulls, so much dust

Ached with near-forgotten form
(a finger, teeth, tongue) – if so,
I shall know only you.

All else washed-clean,
Virgin robes,
Metaphor for the begin-again.

If I am raised, I shall not care if you
Will be like unto severed hand
(Forgetful, free) and I the stump, mourning;

And if, on that day, poetry shall be done
With its need of hearts,
I too shall walk glory-bound,

A Kingdom of Love, I shall
Sing other songs –
Separate and singular, Joy.

Originally published in Rachel Mann,
A Kingdom of Love
(Manchester: Carcanet, 2019)

APPENDIX

A Short and Absurdly Self-Indulgent List of my Parents

IN WRITING THIS book, I very much wanted to avoid a dour scholarly text, overwhelmed with footnotes and references. Nonetheless, some of you might be interested in knowing about a few of the writers, scholars and thinkers who have formed and influenced me. While I shall always be beyond grateful for the love and grace of my birth parents, Shirley and Geoff, there are other parents whose attention and challenge and kindness matter. If my birth parents' greatness is not to be measured in public achievement or book writing, but rather in their character and humanity, there are others who have made and shaped me. This list comprises just a few of the countless 'parents' who have been important to me. Some have been crucial to my intellectual development or literary formation or spiritual growth; some have become friends, while others – if they had been alive to know me – would, I'm sure, have disliked me intensely. This list is not meant to be comprehensive or systematic. Rather, it gives you a flavour of some of the individuals who have made an impact on me. If this book inspires you to do anything, I hope it is to search out their work and read it. So ... in no formal order ...

Ludwig Wittgenstein

I was never much of a philosopher and I fear that, in my youth, I was too readily mesmerised by this great philosopher of Ordinary Language. For several years I was inclined to treat the *Philosophical Investigations* as an almost religious text. Certainly I came to delight in Wittgenstein's exposure of the fakery of so much philosophical enquiry. If I rarely read Wittgenstein now, his attention to the precision and elusiveness of language remains an abiding influence on my writing. His genius lies, in part, in an ability to invite a reader into the mystery at the heart of simplicity.

Judith Butler

I've heard Judith Butler's writing described as 'difficult', 'obscure' and 'disturbing'. It is certainly true that her early work, most famously *Gender Trouble*, requires the most careful attention. I find it is usually only after a Butler-induced headache clears that insight comes. Her claim that 'gender is a copy without an original' is, for me, a key insight. Serially misunderstood, her analyses of gender and sex as well her latter (much more accessible) fascination with politics, grief and precarity remain crucial. A brilliant thinker who has always struck me as fiercely compassionate.

Margery Kempe

The Book of Margery Kempe, written in fifteenth-century England, has been described as the earliest autobiography in English. For me, Kempe is iconic as an example of what Sara Ahmed calls (with great glee and positivity) 'snappy women'. Her story of longing – for holiness, for Jesus, for truth, for life – is, by turns, wild, inspiring, and challenging. Her gift for 'ugly tears' tried the patience of her interlocutors, including several bishops, and she was charged with heresy. Unlike that other medieval female English seeker after holiness, Julian of Norwich, there is nothing refined about Margery. She is an outsider's saint.

Dietrich Bonhoeffer

Bonhoeffer was pretty much the first theologian I read after I came to faith in my mid-twenties. In the midst of what was a quite bewildering and life-altering conversion experience, Bonhoeffer's intelligence, honesty and grip on human failings and grace was leaven. I still go back to *Letters And Papers From Prison*, especially in times of trial. If my theological frames of reference have expanded wildly since that intellectual love affair with Bonhoeffer, he taught me how to be a person of passionate faith who was permitted to use their brain rigorously.

Nicola Slee

I first met Nicola at theological college. Her teaching and friendship opened up the world of feminist scholarship and poetry in ways I could not have anticipated. She was the person who began to show me that perhaps I too might, just might, one day be considered a feminist theologian. Her friendship and kindness has, along with that of other deep and abiding friends, quietly enabled me to see that I am not the useless, unlikeable person I often think I am. She shows me that I too (and people like me) have a place at the table.

Christina Rossetti

Leaving aside Rossetti's most famous poems, I came to Rossetti relatively late. I can see now that her poems and her profound faith had been waiting for me to catch-up for a long time. For all her reputation as a gloomy Victorian, few poets move me so richly or, as in *Goblin Market*, hold the power to reformulate my understanding of the horizons of faith. Feminist scholars have ensured that Rossetti's reputation has been secured in the poetry canon. She now sits at the top table of Victorian poetry. I trust that there she shall remain, though I suspect it would amuse her find herself in the highest rather than 'the lowest place'.

Dorothy L. Sayers

It might surprise some that I include a writer best known for her 'Golden Age' detective fiction. It might further surprise some readers that much as I admire her writings on religion and society and, indeed, adore her fierce public persona, I include her here because of just how much I admire what she could do with genre fiction. If I love Agatha Christie for her deceptive simplicity or John Dickson Carr for his ingenuity, it is Sayers' fiction which has quietly influenced how I think and write. Why? Because for all her early devotion to the rules of detective fiction (she invented a few of them!), she was never afraid to play in the in-between of what was possible. She inspires me to be bolder with genre, as well as with writing more broadly understood. Her great masterwork, *Gaudy Night*, is a detective novel which is as much a novel of manners and a romance; she dares to stretch the lines of genre and generates something greater than we expect. That's something to aspire towards. And, oh, *Gaudy Night*'s ending. Oh, that ending.

Marcella Althaus-Reid

One way of depriving a person or people of voice is to deprive them of language. Marcella Althaus-Reid almost more than anyone has given me the theological language to speak of my experience as a queer woman. If Queer Theology and Theory has moved forward some distance since Marcella died, she was a pioneer. Her ability to make familiar worlds strange remains unsurpassed. Whether in her analysis of the Gospel through the prism of drag or her study of white/western representations of the Blessed Virgin, she deserves to abide.

Jacques Derrida

There was a period where Derrida (or at least versions of him, often crude and simplistic) was so ubiquitous that to mention him as an influence seems like a confession of sin. I need no absolution. If the techniques of deconstruction with which he is synonymous can lead to a rather miserable quietism, it is simply the case that if Derrida hadn't existed someone would have had to invent him. His work on the problem of whether a gift can ever be freely given still haunts me, as does his early work on Husserl. Like Lacan, Irigaray or Kristeva, and indeed all of those thinkers typically dismissed as difficult and dodgy 'Continentals', Derrida's attention to what is suppressed or hidden remains timely. His attentiveness to the nuances of what is hidden when something, anything, is said or written has the character of love (though I suspect he'd have hated being so described). Of course, my openness to Derrida *et al* might simply be an admission that Hegel is much more important to modern thought than most of us should like.

Gillian Rose

Rose is a reminder that one doesn't need to be a former student at the *École Normale Supérieure* to write brilliantly if bracingly into the continental philosophical inheritance. Rose is perhaps most famous now for her extraordinary memoir, *Love's Work*, which explores the reality of cancer and death with minimal sentiment. It deserves its place in the pantheon of memoirs. As a philosopher she wrote primarily about the Law and its implications for our politics and ethics. Her resistance to legalistic understandings of human life and justice – which typically require victims to be in definitive opposition to perpetrators, with a defined winner – challenges our understanding of what it means to live well in the world. She offers ways to resist binaries without ever falling into the temptation of quietism or the nihilism often found in deconstructionist politics. Rose is one of those thinkers who reminds me that I've not thought as deeply as I might about life, the law and the implications of our cultural inheritances. An overlooked giant. She also said the most marvellous things about one of my favourite literary figures, Miss Jane Marple.

Rowan Williams

There's very little I can say about Rowan which would add to his record of brilliance, generosity of spirit and kindness. Perhaps I should simply say that the world is a more hopeful, richer place while he is in it. His openness and warmth towards my work is a token of his generosity.

Jane Howarth

Of all the names on this list, this is the one about whom I think least will be known. Jane was one of my first teachers of philosophy. She believed in me when others didn't and at a time when I believed in myself the least (despite the brittle confidence I sometimes displayed). I shall always picture her with a cigarette in hand, smoke rising in her book-lined rooms, asking questions of me and other undergrads which we barely understood, let alone knew how to answer. She once called me perspicacious. I'm not sure it is still true, but it means a lot to me that once I impressed Jane.

Michael Jagessar

Michael was another of my teachers, this time at theological college. I was inspired by his boldness, his intellectual courage and his – this might surprise you – instinctive naughtiness and disobedience. I've never fully recovered from his poetic-wayward-disruptive liturgical sense, drawn from a deep grounding in the Reformed tradition, in Black Theology, and a childhood in the Caribbean. Few people have challenged me harder to foreground and work through my racism, prejudice and white privilege. Few people have been so permission giving. He reminds me that those days I had at Queen's Foundation in the early noughties were an encounter with some truly sensational and gifted people, including not only Michael, but Stephen Burns, Nicola Slee and Anthony Reddie.

Joan Didion

Didion was the queen of 'New Journalism', that tart and precise form of writing which emerged in Sixties America. She remains a shining example of the power of words in the hands of someone with an off-centre, searching, and wry understanding of reality. Her understanding of the power of a single sentence, well-honed and taut, remains unmatched. Read *The White Album* for her analysis of the collapse of the Sixties' dream, a collapse already inscribed in its white, middle-class aspirations.

John Berger

Ways of Seeing is one of those rare books that holds both revolutionary ideas and re-visions the way in which those ideas are presented. In writing it, Berger enabled a wide audience to encounter Western traditions of art with entirely fresh eyes. Berger was a man who wore his learning lightly, appreciating that teaching is predicated on a kind of gentleness. While he held determined views, I never find his writing dogmatic.

The Traces of Others

I could go on. Rather, here's a short list of others you will certainly find lurking in my writing if you ever decide to take more than a fleeting glance:

A SHORT AND ABSURDLY SELF-INDULGENT LIST OF MY PARENTS

(In no particular order)
Anthony Powell
Donna Tartt
Michael Symmons Roberts
Jean Sprackland
Julia Kristeva
Sharon Olds
Geoffrey Hill
Alain Badiou
Gerard Hughes
John Le Carré
George Eliot
Jane Austen
Sylvia Townsend Warner
Wil Gafney
Evelyn Waugh
Sarah Waters
David Jones
George Herbert
Adrienne Rich
René Girard
Pat Barker
Mary Midgley
J. L. Carr